Message from the author:

The Princess Diaries is a collection of poems shaped by my experiences with various men, some romantic, others not.

Writing has always been my way of making sense of it all, a way to outline the moments that shaped me.

Maybe, in these pages, you'll find a reflection of yourself too.

I hope I inspire you to write, to learn, to reflect, to embrace your own story, to honour your growth, and to see the beauty in both the lessons and the losses.

And most of all, I hope you choose wisely—who you love, who you trust, and who you allow to shape the chapters of your life.

Love,
Princess xoxo

THE PRINCESS DIARIES

Dedicated to all the men that
wonder if I write about them. I do.

THE PRINCESS DIARIES

THE PRINCESS DIARIES

My mind, a storm of thoughts,
crashing, colliding,
no space to breathe,
no pause between the chaos.
They pile, they race,
one on top of the other,
drowning me in the weight
of what I cannot escape.

THE PRINCESS DIARIES

Late nights,
men whispering in my ear,
voices too close,
as if my presence
was a debt to be paid,
as if I owed them
something more
than silence.

THE PRINCESS DIARIES

Him.
Dark eyes, hollow stare,
expecting silence,
expecting me to shrink.
I spat words
watched his mates freeze,
eyes darting anywhere but mine.
Because to look at me
meant they had to choose.
Meant they had to answer.
Meant they had to stand against
him.
And him,
a deer in headlights,
gobsmacked, exposed,
caught between pride and silence,
between the weight of my words
and the eyes of his friends.

THE PRINCESS DIARIES

Tattoos curled over his arms,
spilled across his chest,
reminders, regrets,
pieces of a past
he could never quite leave behind.
A broken man,
wearing his heartbreak
like armor.

THE PRINCESS DIARIES

I searched for the child in him,
the part untouched by pain,
the innocence that once lived
behind his eyes.
But he couldn't find him either.
Violence stole what was his,
grief carved out the rest.

THE PRINCESS DIARIES

THE PRINCESS DIARIES

He admired me like a sunrise,
beautiful, distant,
never to be touched.

THE PRINCESS DIARIES

You spoke with a smirk,
each word a sparring match,
each compliment laced with
condescension.
I hated it,
and yet,
I leaned in closer,
drawn to the sharp edges
of your charm.

THE PRINCESS DIARIES

You learned to live in pieces,
to love like sand slipping through fingers,
never holding too tightly,
never expecting it to stay.

THE PRINCESS DIARIES

"If he wanted to, he would,"
And yet, I lingered,
hoping you'd stay long enough
to prove them wrong.
But actions write truth
louder than words,
and yours were quiet,
absent.

THE PRINCESS DIARIES

THE PRINCESS DIARIES

He did not believe in love,
not in the way I did.
To him, it was purely chance,
rather than destiny.

THE PRINCESS DIARIES

Love doesn't interrupt.
It doesn't forget.
It doesn't make you feel small.
The right man won't run
when you ask for better.
He'll stay,
ready to mend
what broke.

THE PRINCESS DIARIES

The last call came,
brief, fragmented,
it was a mirror of us.

THE PRINCESS DIARIES

In the end,
it wasn't love that failed you.
It was the fear
of letting it stay.

THE PRINCESS DIARIES

THE PRINCESS DIARIES

Kindness does not mean
permission.
A door opened in good faith
is not an invitation to take.

THE PRINCESS DIARIES

At 3 a.m., trust wears thin,
and shadows grow longer.
"No" doesn't echo,
the way it should.
It gets smothered
in the weight of a man's persistence.

THE PRINCESS DIARIES

While I faced the weight of his stare,
his words pushing,
pressing,
breaking the silence.
I didn't sleep.
I couldn't sleep.
I stared at the wall till dawn.

THE PRINCESS DIARIES

Trust is earned,
not assumed.
Kindness is given,
not owed.
And no is enough,
even when it isn't heard.

THE PRINCESS DIARIES

THE PRINCESS DIARIES

He stood his ground,
a man of principles,
even if they were small,
even if they didn't align with mine.
I respected his strength,
but strength without growth
is just stubbornness
wearing a mask.

THE PRINCESS DIARIES

His words found me again,
this time through others.
Lies in the guise of history,
truth bent to wound.

THE PRINCESS DIARIES

She owed me loyalty,
she owed me grace,
but still, she smiled
and took my place.
She didn't love him,
she just wanted
what I once had.

THE PRINCESS DIARIES

Loyalty is a fragile thing,
easily broken,
easily forgotten.

THE PRINCESS DIARIES

*And you don't want to know, how alone
I have been.*

THE PRINCESS DIARIES

THE PRINCESS DIARIES

To him,
I wasn't a person
I was proof.
Proof he could step outside the mould,
touch something different,
and hold it
like a trophy.

THE PRINCESS DIARIES

Names passed like currency,
stories stretched to fit
the weight of their egos.

THE PRINCESS DIARIES

They talk,
as if women are conquests,
names traded over drinks,
stories bent to impress.

THE PRINCESS DIARIES

THE PRINCESS DIARIES

A conversation that felt like home,
a glance that held a promise,
a moment that almost was.
But 'almost' is just a shadow...
never real, never yours.

THE PRINCESS DIARIES

There is no shame in leaving
what never held you.
No defeat in surrendering
what never fought for you.
The only loss
is staying too long at a door
that was never yours to enter.

THE PRINCESS DIARIES

The moon does not weep,
for the tides that leave.
The sun does not mourn,
the night that turns away.

THE PRINCESS DIARIES

THE PRINCESS DIARIES

I found a stranger
who already knew my heart
before I had even named it.

THE PRINCESS DIARIES

You spoke in riddles,
hid behind words,
a presence I could feel
but never fully see.

THE PRINCESS DIARIES

For once,
I was heard.
No fixing,
no judgment,
just space.
I almost mistook it for love,
until I learned
that listening is not the same
as understanding.

THE PRINCESS DIARIES

Some truths are meant to heal,
some to guide.
Yours came with a blade,
disguised as wisdom,
but cutting all the same.

THE PRINCESS DIARIES

He called me spoiled
for wanting softness,
weak,
for asking for kindness.

THE PRINCESS DIARIES

He wrote of love,
of devotion,
of surrendering to fate.
Yet, when I spoke,
he did not listen.
And when I resisted,
he pushed even harder.

THE PRINCESS DIARIES

Some men chase,
not because they love,
but because they cannot bear
to lose.

THE PRINCESS DIARIES

It arrived,
wrapped in pages,
marked with ink,
a love letter in disguise.
All my vulnerabilities,
spilled between the lines.

THE PRINCESS DIARIES

THE PRINCESS DIARIES

THE PRINCESS DIARIES

Men like him
aren't used to being questioned.
A throne built on ego
doesn't take kindly
to someone who refuses
to kneel.

THE PRINCESS DIARIES

He said I failed the test,
as if I had come to him
to seek approval.
As if his validation
was something I wanted,
something I needed.

THE PRINCESS DIARIES

He thought I wouldn't notice,
thought I wouldn't see.
But there he was,
lights flickering,
eyes on me,
timing his steps
like a chessboard move.
And suddenly,
his world shifted
just a little bit closer
to mine.

THE PRINCESS DIARIES

THE PRINCESS DIARIES

You held my book in your hands,
sold it with conviction,
spoke my name with praise.
But was it my words you believed in,
or the chance
that they might lead you to me?

THE PRINCESS DIARIES

I watched the company he kept,
the voices he entertained,
the women who spoke my name
without kindness.

THE PRINCESS DIARIES

A friend does not walk away
when there is nothing left to gain.

THE PRINCESS DIARIES

You never said it,
but I heard it in your waiting.
In the way your hands
carried my name
like it was yours to keep.
In the way your silence
begged for a different answer
than the one I had already given.

THE PRINCESS DIARIES

Water does not beg the stone
to drink.
The sun does not plead with
the sky to rise.

THE PRINCESS DIARIES

THE PRINCESS DIARIES

Yesterday,
he swore against music.
Today,
he hums a tune.

THE PRINCESS DIARIES

The river does not change course
because the mountain wills it to.
It flows where it must,
where the earth bends for it.
No pleading, no prayers,
no waiting at the shore
will turn its waters to you.

THE PRINCESS DIARIES

I do not fear the watcher,
for he watches from a distance.
For a man who must watch
to feel power
is a man
who has none.

THE PRINCESS DIARIES

THE PRINCESS DIARIES

The way he leaned in to listen.
The way he never rushed me.
The way he looked over
like I was the best part of the room.

THE PRINCESS DIARIES

Before I called it love,
I called it peace.
Because that's what he was.

THE PRINCESS DIARIES

He quit his bad habits,
I softened my edges.

THE PRINCESS DIARIES

The rain poured,
but he stood there still,
smoke curling against the cold air.
I stayed too,
drenched, unbothered,
watching him watch me,
half amused, half ashamed.
That night, he flicked the cigarette
away.
Then another.
And another.
Until one day,
there was nothing left
but the memory of smoke
and the rain that washed it away.

THE PRINCESS DIARIES

It wasn't just love
it was the way we laughed.
The way we turned quiet rooms
into places that belonged to us.
The way the world
felt less serious
when we were side by side.

THE PRINCESS DIARIES

One sip,
and the fire rose in him,
spitting embers,
scorching everything in his path.
But I stood untouched.
To me, he was soft,
a whisper in a world of shouting,
a shield where others saw a sword.
The world saw a storm.
I only ever felt the calm.

THE PRINCESS DIARIES

Streetlights flickered past,
soft and distant.
The world was quiet,
except for the low hum of the bike
and the sound of my heart
beating in time
with the speed.

THE PRINCESS DIARIES

I would have fought the world
for him,
stood against the tide, unshaken.
His name,
I would have carved it into the
wind,
let it echo from the rooftops.
I would have walked
until my feet bled,
until the earth itself ran out,
just to stand beside him.

THE PRINCESS DIARIES

He made me believe
love could last forever.
And then,
he showed me it doesn't.

THE PRINCESS DIARIES

I was not mourning him.
I was mourning the girl
who once believed
he was her future.

THE PRINCESS DIARIES

I fixed his life
like it was mine to repair.

THE PRINCESS DIARIES

Simple as this,
we outgrew each other.
Best friends once,
but nothing more.
No anger, no blame,
just time pulling us
in different directions.

THE PRINCESS DIARIES

He kissed new lips,
held new hands,
but the first time he cried in a bar,
it was my name
he sobbed
between drinks.

THE PRINCESS DIARIES

We stood like stone,
stacked strong,
leaning into each other.
Then one piece fell,
and the rest followed,
crumbled into dust.

THE PRINCESS DIARIES

His friends still talk about me,
his mother still texts me,
his name still lingers in rooms
we used to walk through together.

THE PRINCESS DIARIES

THE PRINCESS DIARIES

He walked in like he belonged,
like he had already written himself
into my story.

THE PRINCESS DIARIES

He reshaped his world
to fit me inside it.
Cleared space,
adjusted habits,
became the man
he thought I wanted.

THE PRINCESS DIARIES

I left,
and he barely blinked.
Kept drinking,
kept smoking,
kept chasing silhouettes in the dark,
like love was something
to be won,
not something to be kept.
It was never about me.
Just about the next body
to warm his bed,
the next thrill
to make him forget.

THE PRINCESS DIARIES

THE PRINCESS DIARIES

He spoke like a man
who had seen the world,
who had built something from nothing,
who had walked through struggle
and called it home.

THE PRINCESS DIARIES

Some people are too good for you
not because they are better,
but because their heart
deserves a love
that does not hesitate.

THE PRINCESS DIARIES

People used to say it.
Sometimes, I saw it.
Other times, I ignored it.

THE PRINCESS DIARIES

THE PRINCESS DIARIES

To my face,
he spoke of worry,
of care,
of being different.
But in rooms I wasn't in,
he let the silence speak for him.

THE PRINCESS DIARIES

But jealousy doesn't announce itself
it festers,
quiet, patient,
waiting for a moment
to strike.

THE PRINCESS DIARIES

Whisper it,
and feel the earth shift,
as if even the ground remembers.

THE PRINCESS DIARIES

THE PRINCESS DIARIES

Oh, how much I admired him,
how I wished he'd want me too.
But time unraveled the truth,
it wasn't that he didn't like me,
it was that he couldn't handle me.
Some men admire strength
until it stands beside them,
until it threatens the space
they thought they owned.
And I, unknowingly,
became something to fear.

THE PRINCESS DIARIES

It wasn't that I lacked,
it was that I overflowed.
Too much fire,
too much depth,
too much of everything.

THE PRINCESS DIARIES

I waited.
For a call, a message,
a sign that I mattered.
But silence spoke louder
than any word he never said.

THE PRINCESS DIARIES

Love is not only what is given,
but what is withheld.
It is in the hand that does not reach,
the door that does not open,
the flight that is never taken.

THE PRINCESS DIARIES

THE PRINCESS DIARIES

A hand that grips the air tightly enough, will swear it once held something real.

THE PRINCESS DIARIES

A child sees the world in golden light,
but return with older eyes,
and the shadows tell a different story.

THE PRINCESS DIARIES

I was 14,
wide-eyed, restless,
chasing a dream
that was never mine to catch.
He played guitar,
sang under the stars,
told me to sleep,
worried when I didn't eat.
It was innocent—
at least, it should have been.
Years passed.
And then, he found me.
Said he had been waiting.
Waiting for what?
For time to make me older?
For distance to erase the line
between mentor and something more?
I thought it was fate.
Now, I know better.

THE PRINCESS DIARIES

THE PRINCESS DIARIES

He made faith look easy,
like breathing,
like it was woven into his being.
He answered, never tired,
never laughing at what I didn't know.
He listened, he taught,
and in doing so,
he erased the false images
the world tried to paint.

THE PRINCESS DIARIES

He showed me that belief
was not chains,
but wings.

THE PRINCESS DIARIES

To deserve is to refine,
to polish the soul like a blade
against the stone of patience,
to cleanse the heart
until no filth clings to its chambers.

THE PRINCESS DIARIES

A woman who guards her honor
does not kneel for unworthy hands.
A man who honors his Lord
does not chase fleeting beauty
that wilts in shallow soil.

THE PRINCESS DIARIES

THE PRINCESS DIARIES

They came in waves
some soft, some sharp,
some crashing against the shore of me
and receding like they were never there.
And yet, they left salt in my wounds,
a sting that stayed long after
they had all forgotten my name.

THE PRINCESS DIARIES

There we were,
his eyes, soft, pleading,
asking me to stay.
But his words, sharp as teeth,
pushed me away,
carving distance between us.
The dissonance cut deeper
than silence ever could,
leaving me stranded,
lost between what he wanted
and what he said.
And still, I sat there,
waiting, hoping,
begging for a reason to stay.

THE PRINCESS DIARIES

I sat frozen,
trapped in the space
where truth and fear collide.

THE PRINCESS DIARIES

He called me a "little princess,"
as if the gold in my hands
was not mined from my own spine,
as if the walls around me
were not built from battles I fought alone.

THE PRINCESS DIARIES

THE PRINCESS DIARIES

He stood there,
arms folded like steel,
chin lifted to the sky,
a smile carved from certainty.
Confidence crackled in the air,
demanding not just attention, but respect.
He wasn't loud...
yet the world bent toward him.

THE PRINCESS DIARIES

He smiled
bright, wide, effortless.
The room shifted, drawn to him,
mirroring his every move.
I was caught in his pull,
fixed in place,
like a snake entranced
by the sway of a charmer's tune.
My eyes wouldn't move,
locked in silent defiance,
as if breaking away
meant losing something
I didn't yet understand.

THE PRINCESS DIARIES

My pupils begged for his attention,
looking up...silent, expectant..
like a child waiting to be seen,
to be heard.
His gaze held me still,
comforting, steady,
not in dominance,
not in possession,
but in recognition and love.

THE PRINCESS DIARIES

It was as if I had met
the piece of myself
I never knew was missing.

THE PRINCESS DIARIES

THE PRINCESS DIARIES

I pulled myself in,
arm locked around his,
as if closeness
could shield me
from everything outside of us.

THE PRINCESS DIARIES

"I am sitting in the sun"

"Something tells me you might outshine the sun"

THE PRINCESS DIARIES

THE PRINCESS DIARIES

As if I had met
my own reflection,
not in glass,
but in flesh, in thought, in soul.
Nothing felt forced,
nothing out of place.
He was the answer
I hadn't known I was asking for.

THE PRINCESS DIARIES

The walls crumbled,
the masks fell.
I stood there soft, raw, exposed,
a version of myself
none had seen before.

THE PRINCESS DIARIES

I searched for cracks,
ran my fingers along the edges,
looking for something jagged,
something to call a flaw.
I counted reasons,
stacked them high,
tried to convince myself
you weren't meant for me.

THE PRINCESS DIARIES

I never thought
someone like you
would fit into my world.
Yet the moment I saw you,
even from a distance,
it wasn't a question.
It was recognition,
familiarity in a stranger,
a pull I didn't expect
and couldn't ignore.

THE PRINCESS DIARIES

I craved your presence,
the pull of your space,
the gravity of you.
Every room I entered,
I searched.
For the curve of your smile,
the warmth of your gaze,
the sound of your laugh.

THE PRINCESS DIARIES

You search for the rawest version of me,
not to change,
not to tame,
but to know.
You look at me
like I am something to be understood,
not just admired.

THE PRINCESS DIARIES

To be seen as unforgettable to a man as unforgettable as you.

THE PRINCESS DIARIES

It was the way
he looked at me
as if I was something
worth understanding.

THE PRINCESS DIARIES

A healer gives,
A protector guards,
one softens,
one shields,
a bond of safety,
a love that lasts.

THE PRINCESS DIARIES

They say Allah pairs
the pure with the pure.
And yet, I wonder,
what have I done
to deserve you?

THE PRINCESS DIARIES

"How much do you love me"

"Enough to give up everything for you"

THE PRINCESS DIARIES

THE PRINCESS DIARIES

A stranger's voice,
your betrayal in their hands,
the weight of it pressing down,
heavy, suffocating.
I listened,
but I did not leave.
I questioned,
but I did not run.
Was I the fool for staying?
Or were you the fool
for thinking I never would?

THE PRINCESS DIARIES

THE PRINCESS DIARIES

Words hit like waves,
one after another,
crashing against the walls
I built around you.

Did you think I wouldn't see?
That I wouldn't hear?
That love was enough
to make me blind?

THE PRINCESS DIARIES

I was told things that my heart
refused to hear.
That you were never mine,
that you were never true,
that I should have left
long before now.
Yet I stayed.
Does that make me weak?
Or does that mean I loved
more than you deserved?

THE PRINCESS DIARIES

A thousand thoughts,
none with answers.
Was it real, or just a dream
I convinced myself to believe?

THE PRINCESS DIARIES

Why am I always the one
told to sit in the passenger seat,
to trust the road,
to go along for the ride
without a map of my own?

THE PRINCESS DIARIES

THE PRINCESS DIARIES

I have met men who called me beautiful,
only to say it with hands that took,
with mouths that chewed through my softness
as if I was made to be consumed.

THE PRINCESS DIARIES

I have met men who prayed,
who spoke of God with the same lips
that spoke down to me,
who confused faith with possession,
who thought control was love.

THE PRINCESS DIARIES

I have sat across from men who looked at me like I was something to win,
not something to love.

THE PRINCESS DIARIES

I have seen what it is to be admired
but not known,
to be wanted but not chosen,
to be adored in whispers
but disrespected in the light of day.

THE PRINCESS DIARIES

I have seen betrayal wear familiar faces,
have watched friends fold my secrets
into weapons,
and I have learned that love is not always
a safe place to rest.

THE PRINCESS DIARIES

"You deserve a man who will move mountains for you."
Then they sat still,
hands in their pockets,
as I climbed them alone.

THE PRINCESS DIARIES

I have learned that purity is not about
untouched hands
but an untouched heart
one that refuses to be hardened
by those who could not hold it.

THE PRINCESS DIARIES

That a woman who builds her own castle
has no need for a man
who does not know how to stand beside her.

THE PRINCESS DIARIES

THE PRINCESS DIARIES

I could have turned to stone,
let the weight of
disappointments calcify my
heart,
let their names curdle on my
tongue
like spoiled honey.
I could have carried their
betrayals like heirlooms,
polished my resentment until
it gleamed,
worn my wounds as a
warning,
let my voice sharpen into a
blade.
But I did not.

THE PRINCESS DIARIES

I will not drink the poison of bitterness,
hoping they taste it too.
I will not let anger stain my hands,
or let sorrow chain me to the past.
I will not be made hard by those
who could not hold softness.
I will not become cold
just because they never knew warmth.

THE PRINCESS DIARIES

THE PRINCESS DIARIES

Is it gone?
Is it over?
Listen to the silence,
and there you will find your answer.

THE PRINCESS DIARIES

No conclusions,
no final chapter.
Maybe the real happy ending
is learning to live
without needing one.

www.ingramcontent.com/pod-product-compliance
Lightning Source LLC
Chambersburg PA
CBHW052144070526
44585CB00017B/1968